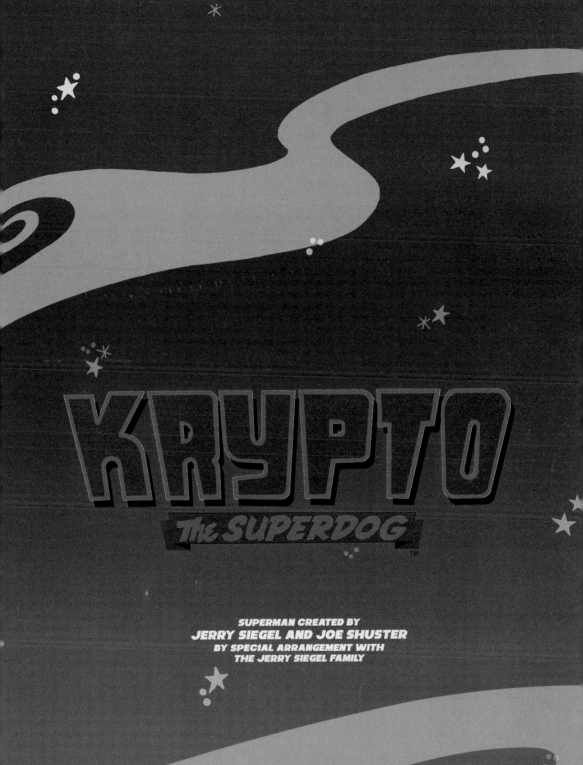

KRYPTO
The SUPERDOG
™

SUPERMAN CREATED BY
JERRY SIEGEL AND JOE SHUSTER
BY SPECIAL ARRANGEMENT WITH
THE JERRY SIEGEL FAMILY

Raintree

Raintree is an imprint of Capstone Global
Library Limited, a company incorporated
in England and Wales having its registered
office at 7 Pilgrim Street, London, EC4V
6LB – Registered company number: 6695582

First published by Raintree in 2014
The moral rights of the proprietor have
been asserted.

Originally published by DC Comics in the
US in single magazine form as Krpyto The
Superdog #3.

Ashley C. Andersen Zantop Publisher
Michael Dahl Editorial Director
Donald Lemke & Sean Tulien Editors
Bob Lentz Art Director
Hilary Wacholz Designer

DC COMICS
Kristy Quinn Original US Editor

ISBN 978 1 406 27952 8

Printed in China by Nordica.
1013/CA21301918
17 16 15 14 13
10 9 8 7 6 5 4 3 2 1

British Library Cataloguing in Publication
Data
A full catalogue record for this book is
available from the British Library.

KRYPTO
The SUPERDOG

Bad Moon Rising

JESSE LEON MCCANN...............................WRITER
MIN S. KU...PENCILLER
JEFF ALBRECHT....................................... INKER
DAVE TANGUAY....................................COLOURIST
DAVE TANGUAY.....................................LETTERER

BAD MOON RISING

WOW, THAT'S A **BIG** MOON TONIGHT!

THAT'S A **HARVEST MOON.** I LEARNED ABOUT IT IN **SCHOOL!**

MANY CULTURES CELEBRATE IT WITH **FESTIVALS** AND **RITUALS.**

LOOKING AT BIG OL' MOONS LIKE THAT MAKES ME **SLEEPY!**

JESSE LEON McCANN – Writer
MIN S. KU – Penciller
JEFF ALBRECHT – Inker
DAVE TANGUAY – Letterer/Colorist
SCOTT JERALDS – Cover Artist
RACHEL GLUCKSTERN – Asst. Editor
JOAN HILTY – Editor

EVERYTHING MAKES YOU SLEEPY, STREAKY, LIKE **SUNNY AFTERNOONS...** OR **RAINSTORMS!**

HA HA HA! OR **TUESDAYS!**

I DON'T SLEEP **THAT** MUCH! CUT IT OUT, YOU GUYS!

SZZZZK! **MECHANIKAT** TO **AGENT N-1**...YOU MAY **BEGIN** YOUR ASSIGNMENT...TZZZT! I REPEAT ...OPERATION **TWIN LIGHTS** IS A GO!

S.T.A.R. LABS
COMMUNICATIONS
DIVISION

DING-DONG!
DING-DONG!

ALL RIGHT,
HOLD YOUR HORSES!
I'M COMING!

EH? *WHO*
RANG THAT
BELL?

MISSION
CONTROL
ROOM

WELL, NOW!
WHO DO WE
HAVE HERE?

PURR!
PURR!

SO, YOUR
NAME IS *NINJA*?
ARE YOU *LOST*,
LI'L FELLA?

MEW!

I'LL TELL *BASE
COMMAND* I FOUND
YOU, NINJA. WE'LL
GET YOU BACK
HOME.

IN THE MEANTIME,
HOW ABOUT I GET
YOU SOME *MILK*?

PURR!
PURR!

LATER...

WELL, *GOODNIGHT*, CREW!
KEEP AN *EYE* ON LITTLE
NINJA FOR ME!

ZZZZZ!

WE WILL,
PROFESSOR.

SOON...

AH! THERE YOU ARE, *AGENT NINJA!* OR SHOULD I SAY...

... *SNOOKY-WOOKUMS!*

THE JOB WAS A *BREEZE*, O WHISKERED ONE, AND *NO ONE* RECOGNIZED ME! THOSE SILLY HUMANS ARE *SO* TRUSTING.

EXCELLENT! PREPARE FOR THE *NEXT PHASE* OF THE OPERATION!

BOY WHAT A DAY! I'M *BUSHED!*

NOT ME! I TOOK A *NAP* EARLI... ER, I MEAN, I PLAN TO STAY UP *LATE* AND GUARD THE NEIGHBORHOOD! NO *SNOOZING* FOR ME TONIGHT!

I JUST WON'T... LOOK AT...THE... *MOOOOON...*

HEY, WHAT'S UP? IS THAT *NORMAL* FOR A HARVEST MOON?

IT'S ALMOST *HYPNOTIC!*

LOOKS LIKE THE *NATIVES* ARE *RESTLESS* TONIGHT!

WE'D BETTER GO SEE WHAT THEY'RE UP TO. *C'MON*, STREAKY!

STREAKY...*HELLO*... CAN YOU *HEAR* ME?

OH, NO! I THINK HE'S BEEN *HYPNOTIZED* BY THE MOVEMENT OF THE *MOON!*

AND I'LL BET *CRAYONS* TO *KRYPTONITE* THOSE *OTHER* CATS ARE HYPNOTIZED, TOO! LOOKS LIKE IT'S *SUPERDOG* TIME!

8

9

OKAY, SO *THAT* DIDN'T WORK.

I'LL HAVE TO GET MORE *CREATIVE!*

A SHORT TIME LATER...

THERE! THAT'S *ALL* OF THEM!

NOW I NEED TO FIND SOME *POLICE OFFICERS* AND *REPORT* THIS.

OH, NO! IT'S A HYPNOTIZED FELINE *EPIDEMIC!*

WHY AREN'T THE *POLICE* DOING ANYTHING ABOUT THIS?

HELLO?! OFFICERS?!

OKAY, THIS SITUATION IS OFFICIALLY *OUT OF CONTROL!*

AND SOMEHOW, THAT CRAZY HARVEST MOON IS *BEHIND* ALL THIS!

TO *FIGURE* OUT WHAT'S GOING ON DOWN *HERE,* I'M GOING TO HAVE TO GO UP *THERE!*

RUFF, RUFF AND *AWAY!*

GASP! THOSE TWO **SATELLITES** ARE CREATING THE SLEEPY EFFECT, **NOT** THE MOON!

I'LL HAVE TO TURN THEM **OFF** THEN, UNTIL THE **SCIENTISTS** FIGURE OUT WHAT? OR **WHO**? DID THIS.

NEGATIVE... YOU...WILL **NOT**.

STREAKY?

MUST...STOP **SUPERDOG**...FROM **BREAKING** SATELLITES.

STREAKY, I'VE **GOT** TO TURN OFF THESE SATELLITES BEFORE THEY CAUSE **MORE** TROUBLE!

YEOW!

REE-REE-REE-REE!

Zap!

TRY TO **CONCENTRATE**, STREAKY! YOU DON'T WANT TO **HURT** ME! WE'RE **BEST FRIENDS**!

MUST... **PROTECT**... SATELLITES.

IT'S *MECHANIKAT'S* SHIP! I SHOULD HAVE KNOWN *HE'D* BE BEHIND THIS!

THAT'S RIGHT, SUPERDOG! I MADE THE SATELLITES *REFLECT* THE MOONLIGHT INTO A *HYPNOTIC BEAM*, CONTROLLING *ALL* THE CATS IN METROPOLIS WITH IT!

WHILE IN A TRANCE, MY *CAT BURGLARS* ARE ROBBING METROPOLIS OF ALL ITS *JEWELS* AND *PRECIOUS ARTIFACTS*, SO THAT I CAN *SELL* THEM THROUGHOUT THE GALAXY!

AND THERE'S *NOTHING* YOU CAN DO ABOUT IT, EITHER, 'CAUSE STREAKY WILL *STOP* YOU!

SHOW HIM WHAT I MEAN, STREAKY!

OOF!

I HEAR... AND *OBEY!*

BAM!

SO LONG! YOU BOYS PLAY *NICE!* HA HA HA HA HA!

OKAY, STREAKY, IF I *HAVE* TO *CONFRONT* YOU, IT'S GOING TO BE ON MY *OWN* TERMS.

SO COME AND *GET* ME, SUPERCAT!

ZZZZZIP!

MUST...*STOP* ...SUPERDOG.

THIS OUGHT TO DO THE TRICK!

-Rrrrip!-

TORO, STREAKY! TORO!

WHOOOOOSH!

FWISSSH!

FWISSSH!

FWISSSH!

THERE, THAT SHOULD *WRAP* THINGS UP NICELY!

RELEASE ME...FOR SUPERDOG...MUST BE... *DESTROYED!*

GEE, I'M *SORRY*, STREAKY, BUT I'VE GOT A MUCH *BETTER* IDEA!

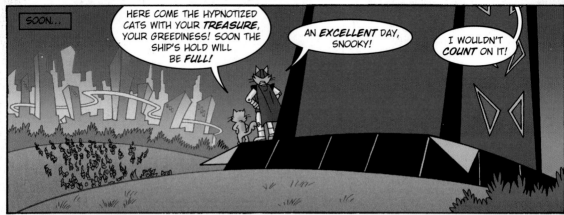

SOON...

HERE COME THE HYPNOTIZED CATS WITH YOUR *TREASURE,* YOUR GREEDINESS! SOON THE SHIP'S HOLD WILL BE *FULL!*

AN *EXCELLENT* DAY, SNOOKY!

I WOULDN'T *COUNT* ON IT!

THAT'S RIGHT. I *UN*-HYPNOTIZED STREAKY BY MOVING THIS SATELLITE BACK AND FORTH, THEN I *RE*-HYPNOTIZED ALL THE CATS TO TAKE ALL THE STOLEN TREASURE *BACK* TO WHERE IT BELONGED!

WHAT? SUPERDOG?

THEN WE SENT THE CATS *HERE,* TO SPEND A LITTLE QUALITY TIME WITH *YOU!*

MEOW.

MEOW.

MEOW!

OH, THIS IS *TORTURE!* PLEASE, *PLEASE* MAKE THEM GO AWAY SO SNOOKY AND I CAN *LEAVE* EARTH!

HELP!

PURR.

PURR.

PURR.

I GUESS WE *COULD* CALL OFF THE CATS...*LATER,* AFTER SUPERCAT AND I TAKE A NICE, LONG *NAP!*

WHAT DO *YOU* THINK, STREAKY?

I THINK IT WOULD BE THE *CAT'S MEOW!*

The END

HEY, *BAT-HOUND*, I HEARD YOU WERE IN *METROPOLIS*! WHAT'S UP?

MY PARTNER *BATMAN* IS VERY BUSY, SO HE SENT ME ON A *SPECIAL MISSION*.

TROUBLE BY THE WADDLE

JESSE LEON McCANN — WRITER • MIN S. KU — PENCILLER
JEFF ALBRECHT — INKER • DAVE TANGUAY — LETTERER/COLORIST
RACHEL GLUCKSTERN — ASST. EDITOR • JOAN HILTY — EDITOR

THAT VILLAIN MOST *FOWL*, THE *PENGUIN*, IS SUPPOSED TO LEAVE THE COUNTRY TODAY. BATMAN WANTS ME TO MAKE SURE HE GETS ON THE PLANE.

"THERE HE GOES. NEXT STOP, *LONDON*."

"LOOK WHO'S GOING ALONG FOR THE RIDE! *ARTIE, GRIFF* AND *WADDLES*, THE PENGUIN'S FEATHER-BRAINED *WINGMEN*!"

"GOOD *RIDDANCE* TO BAD *BIRDIES*."

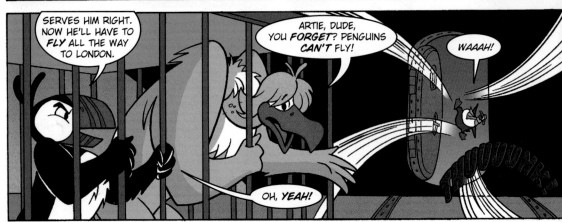

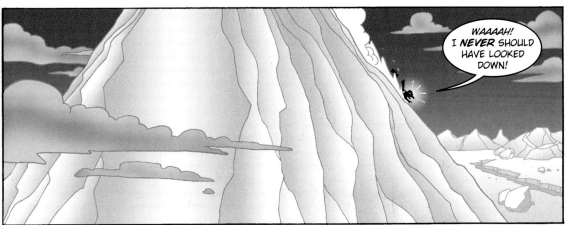

GOOD HEAVENS! YOU'VE TRAPPED ME IN THE *EXPERIMENTAL TUBE* I USE TO TEST *GREEN KRYPTONITE!*

NOW, LET'S NOT *POINT* ANY FINGERS...

SFFPT!

QUICK! YOU HAVE TO GET ME *OUT* OF HERE! PUSH THE *SAME* BUTTON YOU PUSHED BEFORE.

THIS BUTTON?

CLICK!

WAAAAAAAAH!

SKT!

ZAP!

SPARK!

ZZZZPT!

MWAH-HA-HA-HA-HA!

I AM NO LONGER THE *SILLY FOOL* I ONCE WAS. MY *CRAFTINESS* HAS INCREASED A *GAZILLION* TIMES! AND, NOW, FOR MY *FIRST* ACT WITH MY BIG NEW *BRAIN* . . .

... I WILL HAVE MY *REVENGE* ON THOSE MEDDLING DO-GOODERS, *KRYPTO THE SUPERDOG,* AND *ACE THE BATHOUND!* MWAH-HA-HA!

MOMENTARILY ...

INCOMING MESSAGE FROM FORTRESS OF SOLITUDE.

KRYPTO! COME TO FORTRESS OF SOLITUDE RIGHT AWAY! -SUPERMAN.

LOOKS LIKE I'M *NEEDED* UP NORTH! CARE TO TAG ALONG?

WHY NOT? IT'LL GIVE ME A CHANCE TO TRY OUT MY NEW JET-POWERED *BAT-SLED.*

21

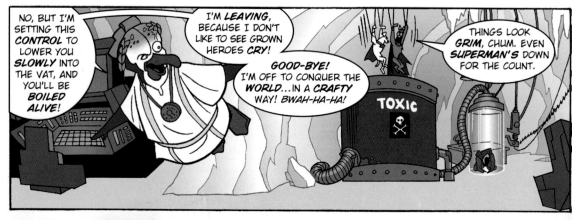

YES, EVERYONE *FLEE* THE CRAFTY WADDLES!

YOUR TOWN IS ONLY THE *FIRST* STOP OF MY WORLD *DOMINATION* TOUR! *MWAH-HA-HA-HA-HA!*

ROARRR!

EEEEEEK!

HELLLP!

AAAAAH!

NOT SO *FAST*, WADDLES!

YOU *CAN'T* TAKE OVER THE WORLD *LOOKING* LIKE THAT!

WHA--?

SSSHOOM!

LET US *SPRUCE* YOU UP A BIT.

SIZZZ!

SPARKZ!

ZAP!

WHAAAAAH!

W-WHAT *HAPPENED?* DID I *REALLY* DO...OOO, I WAS A *BAD* BOY, WASN'T I?

YES, WADDLES, YOU *WERE.*

SUPERDOG AND I HAVE DECIDED THE BEST PUNISHMENT FOR YOU IS TO PUT YOU *BEHIND BARS.*

AND, SO ...

YOU KNOW GUYS, MAYBE IF I'D USED MY *CRAFTINESS* FOR *GOOD,* INSTEAD OF REVENGE AND STUFF, I WOULDN'T FEEL SO *SILLY* NOW!

I THINK YOU MIGHT BE *RIGHT,* WADDLES. I THINK YOU MIGHT BE RIGHT!

TO: LONDON % THE PENGUIN

THE END

Superdog Jokes!

WHAT DO YOU CALL A BOUNCY BREED OF DOG?

A SPRINGER SPANIEL!

WHY ARE DALMATIANS NO GOOD AT HIDE AND SEEK?

THEY'RE ALWAYS SPOTTED!

WHAT DID THE WRITER NAME HIS STORY ABOUT A DEPRESSED DOG?

A VERY SAD TAIL

WHAT KIND OF POOCH PICKS ON OTHER PUPS?

A BULLY-DOG!

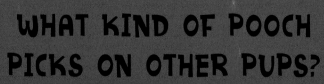

Creators

JESSE LEON MCCANN WRITER

Jesse Leon McCann is a *New York Times* Top-Ten Children's Book Writer, as well as a prolific all-ages comics writer. His credits include Pinky and the Brain, Animaniacs, and Looney Tunes for DC Comics; Scooby-Doo and Shrek 2 for Scholastic; and The Simpsons and Futurama for Bongo Comics. He lives in Los Angeles with his wife and four cats.

MIN SUNG KU PENCILLER

As a young child, Min Sung Ku dreamt of becoming a comic book illustrator. At six years old, he drew a picture of Superman standing behind the American flag. He has since achieved his childhood dream, having illustrated popular licensed comics properties such as the Justice League, Batman Beyond, Spider-Man, Ben 10, Phineas & Ferb, the Replacements, the Proud Family, Krypto the Superdog, and, of course, Superman. Min lives with his lovely wife and their beautiful twin daughters, Elisia and Eliana.

DAVE TANGUAY COLOURIST/LETTERER

David Tanguay has over 20 years of experience in the comic book industry. He has worked as an editor, layout artist, colourist, and letterer. He has also done web design, and he taught computer graphics at the State University of New York.

Glossary

ACQUIRED obtained or got something

ARTEFACT object made by people

DESIST cease, stop, or give up

HYPNOTIC inducing sleep or a trance

PHASE state or step in a process

RESTLESS to find it hard to keep still or to concentrate on anything

RITUAL action or set of actions that are repeated often

TRANCE mental state in which you are not entirely aware of what is happening around you

TRESPASS to enter someone's property without permission

Visual Questions & Prompts

1. EXPLAIN WHAT IS HAPPENING TO STREAKY IN THIS PANEL. WHY DO HIS EYES LOOK THAT WAY?

STREAKY...*HELLO*... CAN YOU *HEAR* ME?

OH, NO! I THINK HE'S BEEN *HYPNOTIZED* BY THE MOVEMENT OF THE *MOON!*

WOO-WOO-WOO-WOO!

1

JOHN'S JEWELS

2. KRYPTO AND ACE MAKE A GREAT TEAM. IDENTIFY A FEW OTHER PANELS IN THIS COMIC BOOK WHERE TWO CHARACTERS WORK TOGETHER.

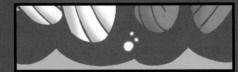

I-I... DID IT...

GOOD JOB, PARTNER. I COULDN'T HAVE DONE IT BETTER *MYSELF.*

2

3. BASED ON WHAT YOU KNOW ABOUT KRYPTO, WHY DO YOU THINK WE CAN SEE THROUGH THE WALL IN THIS PANEL?

LOOKS LIKE THE **NATIVES** ARE **RESTLESS** TONIGHT!

WE'D BETTER GO SEE WHAT THEY'RE UP TO. **C'MON**, STREAKY!

CRASH! THUMP! MEOW. MEOW. MEOW. BANG!

3

4. WADDLES CAN CREATE GREEN CONSTRUCTS WITH HIS MIND. DO YOU KNOW OF ANY OTHER COMICS CHARACTERS THAT CAN DO THIS? WHAT KINDS OF THINGS WOULD YOU CREATE IF YOU HAD THIS POWER?

4